$14 90

DATE DUE

MAR. 18 '98		
OCT 10 '00		
30 505 JOSTEN'S		

CAREERS WITHOUT COLLEGE

COMPUTERS

by Linda Williams

Series developed by Peggy Schmidt

Peterson's

Princeton, New Jersey

A New Century Communications Book

Other titles in
this series include:

CARS
FASHION
FITNESS
HEALTH CARE
MUSIC

Williams, Linda, 1960–
    Computers / by Linda Williams.
        p.   cm.—(Careers without college)
    "A New Century Communications book."
    ISBN 1-56079-224-8
    1. Computers—Vocational guidance   I. Title. II. Series.
QA76.25.W55   1992
004′.023—dc20   92-26694
                                                           CIP

Art direction: Linda Huber
Cover and interior design: Greg Wozney Design, Inc.
Cover photo: Bryce Flynn Photography
Composition: Bookworks Plus
Printed in the United States of America
10 9 8 7 6 5

Text Photo Credits
Color photo graphics: J. Gerard Smith Photography
Page xviii: © Woodfin Camp & Associates, Inc./Chuck O'Rear
Page 18: © Woodfin Camp & Associates, Inc./Sepp Seitz
Page 32: © André Lambertson
Page 48: © AP/Wide World Photos
Page 64: © Woodfin Camp & Associates, Inc./Sepp Seitz

ABOUT THIS SERIES

Careers without College is designed to help those who don't have a four-year college degree (and don't plan on getting one any time soon) find a career that fits their interests, talents and personalities. It's for you if you're about to choose your career—or if you're planning to change careers and don't want to invest a lot of time or money in more education or training, at least not right at the start.

Some of the jobs featured do require an associate degree; others only require on-the-job training that may take a year, some months or only a few weeks. In today's real world, with its increasingly competitive job market, you may want to eventually consider getting a two- or maybe a four-year college degree in order to move up in the world.

Careers without College has up-to-date information that comes from extensive interviews with experts in each field. It's fresh, it's exciting and it's easy to read. Plus, each book gives you something unique: an insider's look at the featured jobs through interviews with people who work in them now.

Peggy Schmidt

ACKNOWLEDGMENTS

Many thanks to the following people for their invaluable assistance in the preparation of this book:

Laura Baijot, Manager of Publishing Operations, Safeco Insurance, Seattle, Washington

James Calloway, Network Operations Manager, Weyerhaeuser Corp., Tacoma, Washington

Bob Hatch, Network Support Manager, Nordstrom, Seattle, Washington

Dave Herarty, Executive Vice President, American Computer Technologies, Metuchen, New Jersey

Michael Kleper, Professor at the National Technical Institute for the Deaf, Rochester Institute of Technology, Rochester, New York

Bill Kubida, Director of Public Relations, MCC/Panasonic, Atlanta, Georgia

Mike Manning, Director of Media Relations, Cleveland Institute of Electronics, Cleveland, Ohio

Jean McKnight, Public Relations Manager, AlphaGraphics, Tucson, Arizona

Lou Mickler, Director of Operations, Eddie Bauer, Redmond, Washington

Blaine Millet, Computer Recruiter, Source Edp, Seattle, Washington

Cindy Ralston, Employment Consultant, Business Careers, Seattle, Washington

Michael Rollins, Desktop Publishing Consultant, Washington, D.C.

Carol Rosen, Chief of Editorial and Publications Division, World Bank, Washington, D.C.

Julia Schroder, Technical Recruiter for Computer People, Inc., Seattle, Washington

John Sparks, Director of Computerland University, Atlanta, Georgia

Steve Unger, Instructor, Lake Washington Technical College, Kirkland, Washington

Bob Williams, Director of Product Training Services, AT&T Technical Training Center, Dublin, Ohio

Dave Williams, Instructor, Silicon Graphics, Mountian View, California

Laura Williams, Public Relations Specialist, Aldus Corp., Seattle, Washington

Linda Peterson, for her editing expertise

WHAT'S IN THIS BOOK

WHY THESE COMPUTER CAREERS?

A few decades ago, the computer industry mainly attracted electronics nuts and nerds because the technology was foreign and difficult for all but the most curious to use. These industry pioneers often built computers from kits in their basements and dreamed of the day when their machines would be faster and capable of running complex applications. Today even preschoolers can use computers to learn the alphabet and create artwork, among other things.

Every time you blink, a faster, more powerful, smaller and less expensive computer hits the market. Each new application of software makes writing, crunching numbers and handling information easier. Computers can now be linked together and to sources of information, making communicating and fact gathering possible on a level unimaginable only a short time ago.

Careers in the computer field can be just as exciting as the machines are. And you no longer have to be a techie to work in the computer industry. In this book you will find five jobs in the computer field. They are:

❏ Computer service technicians—the people who install, maintain and repair computer equipment for manufacturers or service centers
❏ Computer operators—the people who work in data processing centers, directing and monitoring the operations of mainframe computers

❏ Desktop publishing specialists—the people who design and lay out printed materials with publishing software on personal computers

❏ Computer salespeople—the people who sell computers and computer products to individual users and small business owners

❏ Telecommunications technicians—the people who install, maintain and monitor computer networks, which allow computers to talk to one another

These jobs were chosen because none of them requires even an associate degree to get into the field. With the exception of a computer operator, all the jobs do, however, require an interest in and an understanding of how personal computers work, know-how that you may have picked up through taking courses or even learned on your own.

Jobs for technicians—both telecommunications and computer service—are among the fastest-growing jobs in the industry. They're especially worth considering if you are the kind of person who enjoys taking things apart and putting them back together. Acting as a computer "doctor" can be very satisfying, particularly if you work on a regular basis with the end users, the people whose computers and networks you are installing, maintaining and repairing.

For those who are detail oriented and interested in working for employers with minicomputers and mainframes, becoming a computer operator is worth considering. The job is an important one because companies depend on uninterrupted, problem-free use of their computers to process everything from payrolls, to insurance payments, to bank statements.

If you have a flair for things artistic and enjoy working on computers, desktop publishing may be a good option for you. The process involves inputting text and graphics into a computer and working with them to create an attractive final product, which is usually printed material such as a newsletter or brochure, but which could also be a slide show or other visual creation. To become marketable, you have to learn how to use desktop publishing software; if you have graphic design, typography and layout skills to boot, you'll be a hot commodity.

Finally, if you love talking about computers as much as you enjoy working on them, read about what it takes to become a computer salesperson. It's a great way to keep up with the latest in computer hardware and software and offers those with the gift of gab a way to use their talent to make their living.

If you are a quick study, have a "can do" attitude and love the idea of working with computers, you are likely to find success and satisfaction in one of these jobs. Get inspired by what computer game guru Trip Hawkins has to say about making it in the computer industry and how three legendary computer movers and shakers got their starts.

TRIP HAWKINS

on Finding Success in the Computer Industry

Trip Hawkins, 38, is the founder and chairman of Electronic Arts, whose software successes include *Pinball Construction Set*, *Earl Weaver Baseball* and *PGA Tour Golf*. Hawkins always loved to play games, and when he went off to college, he majored in strategy and applied game theory. By the time he was 27 years old, he was head of his own company.

At the time—1982—that was no easy feat, since some 135 other companies were trying to produce and sell computer games. But Hawkins stuck with his vision, and within four years Electronic Arts was the largest supplier of entertainment computer software in the world. Since October 1991 Hawkins has been working on multimedia projects with his new company, SMSG, Inc., which Electronic Arts formed in partnership with Time Warner, Inc.

The computer field is still a new industry, which means that dynamic people who are talented and want to work hard can get ahead. It is a great field to enter because there are some very interesting major new branches of the field. The first branch is wireless communications, a trend that includes not only cellular technology but also communications to devices that are portable and handheld. You can have navigation systems in cars, and you can send faxes to wristwatches.

The second interesting branch is networking, and its potential is just beginning to be realized. And the third is multimedia, which I am involved in. It is interesting from a technological point of view because digital technologies are uniting with traditional forms of film, video and music. There is a real future in that synergy. And the marriage of Hollywood and Silicon Valley will make multimedia an industry that is fun and exciting.

The field has come so far since I first entered it. In my first job in the computer industry, which I had while I was in college, I was a low-level systems analyst for a big mainframe software company called System Development Corp., which was later acquired by Burroughs.

It was there that I realized that I had a place in the computer industry. I was a junior member of a team that was designing a management information system—MIS. One day we had to present the system to the company vice president, who started out the meeting by asking, "Well, what can it do?" The team manager answered, "Well, what do you want it to do?" and they went around and around like that for three hours. I realized that I was the only one who could understand what the system could do and how to bridge the gap between technology and human beings.

I believe if you really want to be in a particular field—
and life is a lot more interesting if you do have a strong
desire for a particular career—you ought to pick the best
organization in that field and take any job in it. You should
even be willing to work for free.

In 1977, when I was in graduate school studying business, I lived down the street from a company called Fairchild, which had the very first programmable video game
system, Channel F. Since I was interested in games, I really
wanted to get my foot in the door there. I offered to do free
market research for them. The price was right for Fairchild,
and I got school credit for it.

Because I had that marketing experience, the next summer I was able to get a job with a market research company,
Creative Strategies. I spent the summer working on a study
of the computer printer market. And after I finished that, I
suggested doing a study of the market potential for the personal computer. (There really wasn't much of a market for
personal computers at the time.)

Apple Computer was just getting started, and as soon
as I finished graduate school, I went to work for them as
the manager of market planning. I eventually became its
marketing manager, and I worked there until I formed
Electronic Arts.

My college and graduate school education probably
helped me to some degree in my career, but I don't think
that kind of education is essential to get ahead in the computer field. You need to be able to communicate, to type,
to write and to spell; you aren't going to get very far if you
don't have those skills. And it helps to have had a computer
at home.

At Electronic Arts I never discriminated against someone because they didn't have a college degree. A lot of
Electronic Arts' best employees did not go to college. Some
of the people we hired were so interested in computers that
they were bored sitting in classrooms and never went on
for further education. They were valuable to Electronic
Arts because they were instinctively familiar with the char-
acter of the media: they knew how to develop computer
programs and how to market them. They understood the
people who would buy the software.

I can think of two people at Electronic Arts who went far without college degrees. One guy is vice president for Electronic Arts Studios. He is 31 years old and has been with the company for nine years. Another employee is director of marketing for Electronic Arts' European business, which has annual sales of about $60 million. He didn't even finish high school, and he's been with Electronic Arts for ten years—since he was 18. The computer industry was fun for him, and he made himself real familiar with it. He had taken a lot of personal time to learn about the field—he spent time in stores, going to trade shows and thinking about the business and how to make it better.

I am impressed by people who are willing to put the success of the company ahead of their personal interests. The most important common ingredients for people in the field are desire, determination, willingness to work hard and being good team players. There are many jobs in the computer industry for people with those qualifications.

FAMOUS BEGINNINGS

William H. Gates III, Chairman and CEO of Microsoft Corp., Redmond, Washington

While in high school, Gates worked in the mainframe and minicomputer programming field. In college he worked with Paul Allen to develop the BASIC programming language for the first commercially available microcomputer, the MITS Altair. He and Allen went on to form Microsoft Corporation. The company has been so successful—in part, due to its top-selling *Windows* software and the *OS/2* operating system—that, according to a *New York Times* article, over 2,000 of the company's employees are estimated to be millionaires. And Gates, 36, is reputed to be the wealthiest man in America.

Steven P. Jobs, Cofounder of Apple Computer, now President and CEO of NeXT Computer in Redwood City, California

In college Jobs landed a summer job at Hewlett-Packard. He dropped out of school, lived on a commune harvesting apples (which gave him the inspiration for his company name) and experimented with the video game field. His timely hook-up with Steve Wozniak, who had built a computer in his garage, resulted in their marketing the computers for $666.66 each. The rest, as they say, is history. In late 1985, after leaving Apple, Jobs cofounded NeXT Computer, Inc., to design, manufacture and market professional workstations.

Paul Brainerd, age 45, Founder and President of Aldus Software, Seattle, Washington

Brainerd worked as a teaching assistant in photography at the University of Oregon. As a graduate student in journalism at the University of Minnesota, Brainerd worked on the student newspaper and helped modernize its printing process. After graduating, he helped the *Minneapolis Star and Tribune* switch to a modern production process as well. He later worked for Atex, a manufacturer of computerized publishing equipment. Founding Aldus, which brought desktop publishing to personal computers, was a logical step to Brainerd. In 1991 Aldus, best known for its *PageMaker* software, had sales of $167 million.

XV

There are many people who believe that the two scariest words in the whole English language are "System Error." What do they do after their monitor screen freezes with that chilling message? If they can't solve the problem themselves, they'll probably call in a "computer doctor"—a computer service technician.

With millions of computers installed in offices, hospitals, schools and homes, the demand for computer service technicians is strong: it's the second-fastest growing career area in the computer industry, second only to system analysis (which requires a college degree).

Computer service technicians (who are also called field, customer or service engineers, among other things) install

1

equipment, upgrade computers by installing drives, cards and new motherboards and do preventive maintenance such as cleaning and replacing worn parts and diagnosing problems. Of course, they're really in their element when something goes wrong and a user or an entire department is "on hold" until the problem can be solved.

Some computer service technicians work on personal computers brought in by customers to retail stores and repair shops. Others work for end users, that is, companies and organizations that have mainframe or minicomputer systems that must be in good working order at all times. Among the biggest employers of technicians are insurance companies, banks, hospitals and financial services firms. Still others work for computer manufacturers who offer service contracts to their customers. These technicians usually specialize in installing and repairing the computers manufactured by their employer. And finally, some work for third-party maintenance organizations, which service the computers of client companies.

If you're fascinated by computers and have always enjoyed the fun and challenge of taking things apart and putting them back together, maybe you can get paid to do it as a computer service technician.

What You Need to Know

❑ Basic understanding of computer operating systems (*DOS, System Files, OS-2*); hardware (IBM and IBM compatibles, Apple and Hewlett-Packard peripherals); software (word processing, spreadsheet and database programs)
❑ How components (hardware) in a particular computer system fit together
❑ Current computer design, circuitry and architecture (the processing speed of a microprocessor, the amount of memory)
❑ The purpose of different components on a computer's motherboard
❑ Basics of electronics circuitry (currents, voltages and resistance)
❑ How semiconductors work
❑ Basic computer arithmetic (how the computer "thinks" in zeros and ones) and digital codes such as ASCII
❑ Basic mathematics (to calculate processing speeds and memory capabilities)

Necessary Skills

❑ Ability to wire components together
❑ Soldering
❑ Facility with tools such as screwdrivers
❑ Good listening and verbal skills (you need to pay close attention to the problem as described by a customer and ask good questions)
❑ Strong reading and comprehension skills (equipment is changing constantly, and you have to read and refer to manuals to keep up to date)

Do You Have What It Takes?

❑ Ability to listen and ask questions of users about equipment problems

❑ Ability to sort through such information and make logical deductions as to the cause of a problem

❑ Powers of concentration that allow you to stick with a problem until you solve it

❑ Good powers of observation (to detect loose connections, worn or defective parts)

❑ Tolerance for dealing with people who are irate, frustrated or unhappy because their computer is not working

❑ A soothing disposition (you have to be reassuring and cool as a cucumber in dealing with users in distress)

Physical Attributes

❑ Manual dexterity (be able to handle and work with small pieces of hardware and tools)

❑ Strength (you must sometimes pick up equipment that may weigh up to 80 pounds)

Education

A certificate of completion of a one-year program in computer hardware repair from a vocational or technical school or an AAS (Associate in Applied Science) in electronics engineering technology from a two-year community college or correspondence school is recommended but not necessary.

Licenses Required

Several states, including Oregon, California, Connecticut and Louisiana, require electronics technicians to be certified by the International Society of Certified Electronic Technicians. Some employers prefer hiring certified technicians, even if certification is not required by the state.

Technicians who specialize in a specific manufacturer's equipment may be required to earn certification on that company's products before they can work on machines without supervision. Certification may require taking a course at a regional office of the manufacturer, or home study, using the manufacturer's manual in preparation for an exam.

◆ **Job Outlook**

Job openings are expected to grow: much faster than average

Jobs in computer service are predicted to increase by 60 percent between 1990 and 2005—from 84,000 to 156,000 jobs. That's because more and more individuals and businesses will be using computers, which will need maintenance and repair.

◆ **The Ground Floor**

Entry-Level Jobs

❑ In-house repair technician (works for end users in the MIS or data processing department or in repair department of a retail computer store). Beginners are often called bench technicians because they spend their time doing small repairs on computers and peripherals at the bench rather than doing maintenance and repair at the site of the computer.
❑ Computer field service and support technician (works for computer manufacturer or third-party maintenance organization and travels to offices, schools or homes to service or repair computer equipment).

◆ **On-the-Job Responsibilities**

Beginners

❑ Install computers by connecting components, wiring units to electrical outlets and testing the units to make sure they work correctly
❑ Service machines by cleaning parts and connections, lubricating movable parts, replacing worn keys on a keyboard or parts of a printer and making adjustments for print quality on printers or on monitor screens

❑ Repair machines by performing diagnostic tests or analyzing from user complaints what is wrong, then replacing or repairing the necessary parts

❑ Keep records of routine maintenance and repairs, track parts used and order replacements

❑ Run special programs to force the system to run at peak capacity (a preventive maintenance routine)

Experienced Technicians

❑ All the above, plus supervise and advise less experienced technicians

When You'll Work

Technicians who work in a retail store's repair shop often work nine to five, five days a week. They may also work one weekend day and on federal holidays when the store is open.

Technicians who work for end users who keep typical office hours often keep the same hours themselves. They may, however, also work after hours or on weekends or holidays when installing new equipment, doing routine maintenance or upgrading the network.

Technicians who work for companies that require around-the-clock network monitoring must sometimes work or be on call on late night (3 P.M. to 11 P.M.) shifts. Working an overnight shift (11 P.M. to 7 A.M.) is unusual, but if you work it, you usually are paid at a higher rate or can elect to get comp time (extra time off). The same is true if you work overtime, on weekends or holidays. Newcomers are the most likely ones to get stuck with undesirable hours. Part-time work options are rare.

Field service technicians usually carry beepers so they can be contacted around the clock by clients of their company who are experiencing computer problems.

Time Off

Vacation, paid holidays and sick days depend on the type of employer.

Technicians who are employed by large companies generally receive the same vacation allowances as other employees, which tend to be more generous than those of retail stores and third-party maintenance organizations, which are small businesses.

❑ Discounts on computers, components or software sold by the manufacturer or retail store you work for
❑ Use of a company car (available for some field service technicians)

◆ **Perks**

❑ Retail computer stores
❑ Computer repair shops
❑ Computer manufacturers
❑ End users (any company, hospital or organization that uses computers or computer systems)
❑ Third-party maintenance organizations (who service the computers of a number of company clients)

◆ **Who's Hiring**

❑ The possibility of shocks from electrical equipment (if safety precautions are not observed)
❑ Potential for back trouble from lifting equipment
❑ Minor cuts from tools or sharp metal edges
❑ Exposure to chemicals such as printer toner

◆ **On-the-Job Hazards**

Beginners and experienced technicians: little potential for travel.

The exception is field service technicians. Travel for them may be local or it may require covering a region. Large companies may have technicians based in locations around the country, while smaller ones may expect employees to travel as much as 50 percent of the time. Travel schedules are rarely routine. When a remote computer breaks, the technician will hop in a car or airplane to get to the site as soon as possible.

◆ **Places You'll Go**

Computer service technicians work wherever computers are found. Mainframe and minicomputer systems are often located in rooms without windows. Personal computers, of course, are found in all types of offices and work spaces,

◆ **Surroundings**

from an elegant executive suite to a spare desk in a tiny office overlooking a manufacturing area. Repair shop environments are often filled with shelves of spare parts, workbenches cluttered with tools and computer parts, and floors scattered with boxes and large machines.

Dollars and Cents

Technicians generally start at $7 to $10 an hour. A technician with five years' experience will probably earn between $25,000 and $45,000. Top technicians can have earnings approaching six figures. Longer than average work weeks at time-and-a-half earnings help keep service technicians' earnings high.

Moving Up

You might start off as a bench technician and, with experience and a track record of being terrific at what you do, get promoted to head technician. Ace technicians often earn the job title of technical analyst or specialist.

The best way to move up is to keep up with the latest changes in the equipment you regularly work on. If you work for an end user, you will probably be able to do this by going to seminars offered by the manufacturers of the equipment used in your company, often on company time. You can increase your marketability by learning how to service other types of computers on your own time.

If you work for an end user with extensive servicing needs and you prove yourself to be an ace technician with management potential, you may head up the technical repair team. However, you will probably still report to the head of data processing or MIS. If you work for a computer manufacturer, with years of experience and the right leadership qualities, you may also be promoted to head up the field service technician staff.

Where the Jobs Are

Wherever there are computers, there is work for computer service technicians. End users and retail computer stores can be found everywhere in the country, although the biggest ones are more likely to be found in major metropolitan areas.

Computer repair and electronics programs are offered by community colleges, technical institutes and sometimes even by vocational/technical high schools. You can earn a diploma in electronics technology or an Associate in Applied Science (AAS) degree in electronics engineering technology. For lists of accredited schools in your area, contact the American Society for Engineering Education (11 Dupont Circle, Suite 200, Washington, D.C. 20036). You can find out about take correspondence courses that are accredited through the National Home Study Council (1601 18th Street N.W., Washington, D.C. 20009).

Education Information

Between 60 and 70 percent of computer service technicians are male. However, as women have been gaining more exposure to computers in school, more are likely to consider computer repair a good job choice.

The Male/Female Equation

Making Your Decision: What to Consider

The Bad News

- ❑ Low starting salary
- ❑ Working under time pressure
- ❑ Having to deal with unreasonable demands or expectations from clients
- ❑ Lots of unrewarding grunt work
- ❑ Work is usually behind the scenes, with little recognition

The Good News

- ❑ Good salary (if you have experience)
- ❑ Overtime pay
- ❑ Job security
- ❑ Not being confined to the same work environment (for field repair technicians and those who work for third-party maintenance organizations)
- ❑ Demand for skills likely to remain strong

More Information Please

IEEE Computer Society
1730 Massachusetts Ave. N.W.
Washington, DC 20036-1903
202-371-0101

IEEE represents every segment of the computer science and engineering community. The $57 membership fee includes a monthly subscription to *Computer Magazine*. Job listings are also made available to members.

International Electronic Technicians Association
602 N. Jackson
Greencastle, Indiana 46135
317-653-8262

This association provides certification for electronic technicians at four levels: associate ($20 for the exam), journeyman ($30), senior ($50) and master ($75). The exams can be administered by representatives around the country. Membership ($32 a year) includes the monthly newsletter *Electronic Technician*.

International Society of Certified Electronics Technicians
2708 West Berry Street
Fort Worth, Texas 76109
817-921-9010

The society, called ISCET, offers certification tests for $25, which are required by several states and some employers. Electronics technicians who become certified can join ISCET ($25 a year) and receive the quarterly newsletter "Update" and the bimonthly magazine *Professional Electronics*.

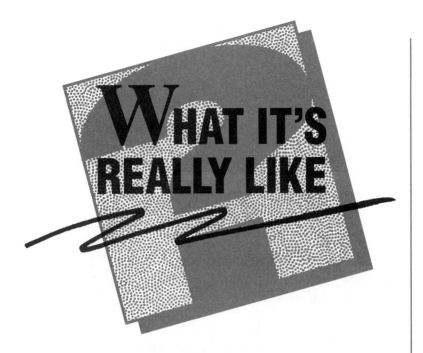

Michael Holtz, 27,
technical analyst,
The Toledo Hospital,
Toledo, Ohio
Years in the business: seven and a half

How did you break into the field?
I started as a bench technician in one of the Abacus II computer stores in Toledo, working under the head technician. I repaired Apple and IBM computers and peripherals that people bought in the store or that came from other stores. We usually replaced the parts that weren't working, then sent out the broken ones to another company that repaired them.

Was it a typical first job?
Very typical. I learned a lot at that job.

What kind of preparation did you have for it?
I went to the Total Technical Institute near Cleveland for a nine-month certificate program in computer hardware repair. Afterward I sent resumes to all the shops and businesses in Toledo that I thought would need repair technicians.

11

What was the hardest aspect of working in the field during your first few years?

The hardest part was learning the functions of PCs. I learned at the technical school how to repair them, but not how to boot up software. I didn't know, for example, that *Lotus 1-2-3* (a spreadsheet program) takes up X amount of memory, so if someone is having problems with their computer, it could be that there isn't enough memory left to run the program, and not that there's a problem with the hardware at all.

How long did it take you to get established?

It took about a year for me to feel comfortable. My bosses must have thought that, too, because after a year and a half they sent me to another one of the stores as head technician.

How many different jobs have you held in the field?

Four. At Abacus II I was a bench technician, a head technician and a field service technician. Now I'm a technical analyst.

What do you currently do?

I'm the only one in the hospital who maintains the PC hardware; I don't deal with mainframes. I maintain between 550 and 600 computers, mostly IBMs and clones. I hook LANs (local area networks) together, order equipment, unpack and set up computers and peripherals, install operating systems, change motherboards when they aren't working correctly, take care of floppy drive and printer problems and swap any part that is broken or causing a hardware problem.

What do you like most about your work?

I like helping the people. At Abacus, I might have helped someone and never have seen that person again. At the hospital, I don't have irate customers; I don't have to give them bills. It's nice to see the people later and to know that they appreciate you. I like the feeling of being needed.

What do you like least?

I like doing the repair—but I have trouble finding the time to do it all. Sometimes I can't answer phone messages until a day later. I don't like it when I get too busy and I can't respond quickly enough to people's problems.

What has been your proudest achievement?
I like the fact that I've been able to reach the status that I'm at now, and that I've been able to stick with it. I'm married and have two kids. We live in a nice house, and I'm happy to be able to support them doing what I do.

What advice would you offer someone who's thinking about entering this field?
You're going to need some kind of education or training for this job. You need experience, either from a technical school or volunteering for a company and working for free as you learn.

Joe Henderson, age 52,
computer systems engineer,
The Computer Store,
Mukilteo, Washington
Years in the business: one and a half

How did you break into the field?
When I was still driving trucks, I hurt my back lifting a keg of beer on a job. I had to have two back surgeries after that, and the doctor said I could never drive a truck again. So while I was at home recuperating, I started fiddling with my wife's IBM computer clone and taught myself how to type. I always liked to see how things worked when I was a kid, and then I started thinking, maybe I could learn how computers work. So I went to tech school and learned.

One of my teachers specialized in Macintoshes, and I really enjoyed working with them. So when I finished school, I called the service manager of The Computer Store, which sells only Apple equipment. The manager had been through the same tech school six or seven years before, and he gave me a job.

What did you do on your first job?
As soon as I started, they showed me how to swap logic boards and said, "Okay, now get to work." I repaired Apple computers, printers and monitors, most of which had been bought in the store and were still under warranty. Af-

ter a few months, I started specializing in laser printers. I just sat down and said, "Now let's figure out how these things work."

Was it a typical first job?
In terms of what I did, the job was typical, but for the salary, no. Not too many of my classmates took jobs with pay this low. I started out at $6 an hour, and not too many people could afford that low a wage.

What kind of preparation did you have for it?
I went to a vocational tech school. Since then I've studied on my own to be certified on GCC laser printers and Radius monitors, and soon I'm going to get certified on the Apple product line.

What was the hardest aspect of working in the field during your first few years?
The hardest part at first was trying to help customers over the phone when I wasn't really sure what was wrong or how to fix it. I didn't like putting them on hold and asking a co-worker questions. If I could see the machine, I could understand it, but trying to visualize what the customers were trying to explain, when they sometimes had no idea what they were talking about, was hard.

How long did it take you to get established?
It took me about four months to feel comfortable, and about a year and a half to feel established. I just got my first promotion and my second pay raise.

What do you currently do?
I just started going out and doing on-site repairs, especially for laser printers.

What do you like most about your work?
I like the challenges most—the challenge of solving the problem. Working with each new machine that comes up has unique problems, which is great because I love to learn and hate to be bored.

What do you like least?
The disorganization in our service department right now really bothers me. We don't always have the right parts because we need to increase our inventory, and parts are scattered all over the department. We're going to change it

so that all the laser printer stuff will be at my bench, and there will be separate sections for ImageWriter stuff, computer stuff, etc.

What has been your proudest achievement?
My proudest achievement was that I was just promoted to systems engineer. I still primarily do repairs, but now I can go on site and handle some corporate clients.

What advice would you offer someone who's thinking about entering this field?
My advice is to read and learn about all different types of hardware, operating systems and software. You are only limited by the limitations you place on yourself. You just have to find a little niche and fill it, and then you can become another Bill Gates.

Dan Thacker, 32,
regional head of field service, NCUBE,
San Mateo, California
Years in the business: 12

How did you break into the field?
When I was in the Marines, I learned basic electronics; I learned how to fix 1950s radios. Then in 1978, after I had left the service, I got a job working on Radio Shack computers for a company called Micro Technology Inc. When I started, my boss told me I had 30 days to show a profit. I had to learn a lot on my own.

What did you do on your first job?
The company took Radio Shack computers, upgraded them and resold them. We were expanding their displays from 64 columns to 80 by adding boards, we were adding RS-232 boards and we were adding double-sided disk drives. We were building some of the components ourselves and installing them in the computers.

Was it a typical first job?
I guess it was typical. It was your basic job-shop type place.

What kind of preparation did you have for it?
In the military I had two years of eight-hours-a-day electronics school. It covered basic mathematics, basic electronics, digital logic and 18 weeks of ground radio repair. After that I mostly taught myself about computers. I did a lot of reading—books and magazines like *Byte*—and I bought a Radio Shack computer so I could teach myself how to program in BASIC.

What was the hardest aspect of working in the field during your first few years?
The constant change was the hardest part at the beginning. There were a lot of little companies that were very volatile, so I was always trying to stay one step ahead of a company folding. Or I was trying to be a cut above my co-workers so that if the company had layoffs, they would keep me. But I had to change jobs every six months anyway, so I could keep increasing my wages and get more experience.

How long did it take you to get established?
It took about five or six years, because I started out at the bottom, at $5 an hour. After about five years, I was doing western region technical support for a company called ELXSI, and I was making about $50,000 a year.

How many different jobs did you hold in the field?
I guess I've had about ten jobs. I was in field service for about seven years, in design engineering for five years and in computer repair for two and a half years.

What do you currently do?
I'm manager of western region technical support for a company called NCUBE. It makes massively parallel (8192-processor) machines. I'm in charge of preventive maintenance, service and repair for about 50 machines that are in the region, plus the machines that are in our offices. I install machines for our software developers, review new designs and repair the computers. I have to do some international travel to service machines, too.

What do you like most about your work?
I like the diversity—every day is different. If it gets too hectic in the office, I can always book a trip somewhere to do preventive maintenance on a machine.

What do you like least?

The pace never slows down. You have a lot of people and responsibilities making demands on your time, so you feel like you're on a leash. About a month ago, I was told at 10 A.M. that I had three hours to get ready for a flight to Germany, where I had to fix a computer. I can get calls at home at midnight, because our computers run around the clock all over the world. That's especially tough because I have a family.

What has been your proudest achievement?

My proudest achievement is the ability to be compensated well for the work I do, without having that piece of paper—a college degree. I started at $5 an hour, and in the beginning I had to keep switching jobs to get $2 an hour raises. Now I'm earning about $86,600 a year. The amount of money I make is extraordinary, but I credit it to being in the right industry at the right time. To increase my salary at the rate I did, I changed jobs as often as every six months. Fortunately, I was able to convince each employer that I was worth the salary I was asking.

What advice would you offer someone who's thinking about entering this field?

I'd say don't go in expecting to work for one company for the rest of your life. You have to want to move around and keep learning, because that's the only way you'll increase your salary, and the only way to get experience on many different platforms. I'd also say that you don't need to have a college degree to get ahead. The machines that people are learning on today at universities are already outdated—they don't have massively parallel machines like the ones I work on.

Behind every large company stand powerful mainframe computers that maintain records, process financial data and organize information. During the past 20 years businesses have learned there is practically no limit to a mainframe's capabilities. But computers are, after all, only as good as the people who operate them. These people, computer operators, are the unsung heroes of data processing departments.

They load tapes into drives according to a complicated, fast-paced schedule, enter commands to run specific "jobs," separate printout pages and deliver them to people in the department and end users throughout the company and report any

19

problems with the machines or the programs running on them.

Computer operators work behind the scenes, but they are integral to their company's data processing operation. If a mistake is made, the computer may begin producing the wrong job, information may get printed on the wrong forms or the equipment may go down if commands are not executed precisely. Lost computer time or productivity can turn a data processing center on its ear, which is why it's so important to follow instructions exactly and pay great attention to detail.

Computer operators can find employment in a wide variety of settings. Manufacturing firms rely on the machines to track parts ordering, storage and delivery. Department stores use computers for inventory and supply, order shipments and customer account information. Banks count on computers for account balances, financial transactions, stock market news and funds data. And almost every large-sized company needs mainframes for financial records, employee benefits and payroll information.

Being a computer operator is one of the best ways to get a foot in the door of a company, learn about its business and get hands-on experience with powerful computers. If you think that's where your foot would like to go, it may be a step worth taking.

What You Need to Know

◆ **Getting into the Field**

❑ Computer terminology
❑ The basics of how mainframe computers operate

Necessary Skills

❑ A logical, problem-solving mentality (so you can figure out what went wrong before having to contact your boss)
❑ Ability to follow oral or written instructions precisely
❑ Good verbal skills (so you can describe operations and problems)
❑ Good reading and comprehension skills (so you can understand step-by-step procedures)

Do You Have What It Takes?

❑ Ability to work with little supervision
❑ Ability to work well under stress
❑ Interest in and no fear of mainframe computers

Physical Attributes

❑ Strength (you may be required to lift computer components and boxes of pre-printed forms)

Education

Nothing beyond a high school education is required.

Licenses Required

None

Job openings will grow: more slowly than average

◆ **Job Outlook**

After fast growth during the eighties and early nineties, jobs for computer and peripheral operators will increase more slowly than most other jobs in the computer industry. It is estimated that there will be 361,000 jobs for computer operators in 2005, an increase of 13 percent over 1990.

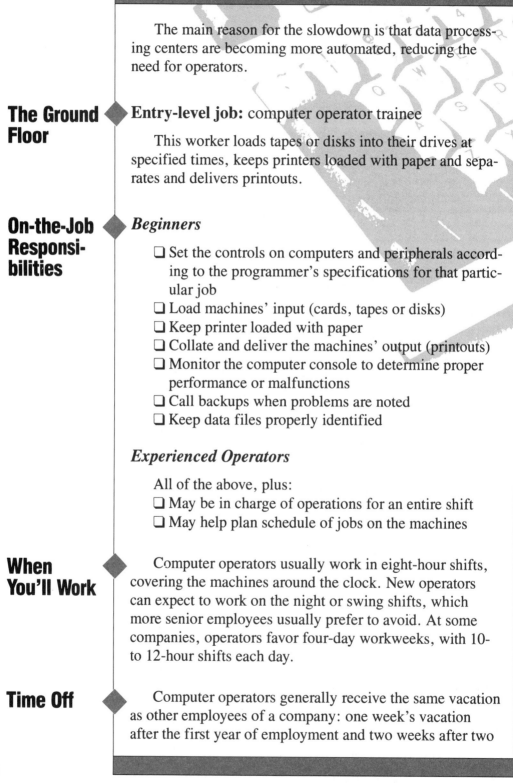

The main reason for the slowdown is that data processing centers are becoming more automated, reducing the need for operators.

The Ground Floor

Entry-level job: computer operator trainee

This worker loads tapes or disks into their drives at specified times, keeps printers loaded with paper and separates and delivers printouts.

On-the-Job Responsibilities

Beginners

❏ Set the controls on computers and peripherals according to the programmer's specifications for that particular job
❏ Load machines' input (cards, tapes or disks)
❏ Keep printer loaded with paper
❏ Collate and deliver the machines' output (printouts)
❏ Monitor the computer console to determine proper performance or malfunctions
❏ Call backups when problems are noted
❏ Keep data files properly identified

Experienced Operators

All of the above, plus:
❏ May be in charge of operations for an entire shift
❏ May help plan schedule of jobs on the machines

When You'll Work

Computer operators usually work in eight-hour shifts, covering the machines around the clock. New operators can expect to work on the night or swing shifts, which more senior employees usually prefer to avoid. At some companies, operators favor four-day workweeks, with 10- to 12-hour shifts each day.

Time Off

Computer operators generally receive the same vacation as other employees of a company: one week's vacation after the first year of employment and two weeks after two years. However, they often need to work on holidays, when the machines can be relieved from day-to-day duties and run large processing jobs.

Any user of mainframe computers, including:
- ❏ Banks
- ❏ Manufacturers
- ❏ Retail and wholesale companies
- ❏ Computer firms
- ❏ Insurance companies
- ❏ Financial services companies
- ❏ Colleges and universities
- ❏ Utility companies (telephone, electric, oil and gas)
- ❏ Government agencies
- ❏ Service bureaus (that process mainframe jobs for a number of clients)
- ❏ Hospitals

◆ **Who's Hiring**

Beginners and experienced operators: little potential for travel.

◆ **Places You'll Go**

Computer operators work in environments that are suitable for mainframe computers: air-conditioned, well-ventilated and artificially lighted (no windows) spaces. Data processing centers usually hum with the sound of equipment.

◆ **Surroundings**

Computer operators almost always work for hourly wages. Beginners earn between $6.50 and $11 an hour, while those who have been in the field for five years or more can expect to be paid $10.50 to $15 an hour. Computer operators who advance to positions of greater responsibility—some as supervisors—can earn $15 to $21 an hour. Night pay is usually higher and is called shift differential. Working holidays usually means getting paid on a time-and-a-half basis.

◆ **Dollars and Cents**

Moving Up

Although computer operations was once a way to start climbing a career ladder within the computer world, now it rarely is. In most places computer operators cannot move up to any job beyond supervising other operators unless they go back to school to get a degree in computer science or management information systems (MIS).

Where the Jobs Are

Any area that boasts a large number of mainframe users (the case with all major metropolitan areas) employs computer operators.

Schooling

Training is done on the job because job tasks can be quickly learned and each is somewhat unique to the operations of a particular company's data processing center.

The Male/Female Equation

The current ratio is about 60 percent men to 40 percent women.

Making Your Decision: What to Consider

The Bad News

❑ Job tasks are repetitious
❑ Long or night shift work often required
❑ No career path upward (in most companies)
❑ High pressure when malfunctions occur

The Good News

❑ Work with little supervision
❑ Casual dress code
❑ Listen to music (radios and tape decks are often permitted in data processing centers)
❑ Play a vital role in company operations

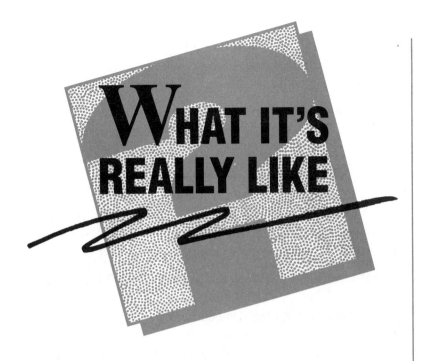

WHAT IT'S REALLY LIKE

Audrey Hollingsworth, 25,
input/output rover, Nordstrom,
Seattle, Washington
Time in the business: three months

How did you break into the field?
I'd been looking for a job for a few months, and I ran into someone I knew who had just started working in data processing at Nordstrom. He told me about a job opening and then recommended me for it.

What do you do?
I work in the data processing center, mounting tapes according to a schedule. We do a lot of filing in the tape library. I work nights now, but every morning the day crew has to pull between 600 and 800 tapes from a vault. We ship them off to make copies for backups, and in two days we get the originals back. The copies are sent to California for safekeeping. We also pull about 2,000 scratch tapes a day from the library—those are tapes that can be written over.

When I have time, I also do some work on the computer.

For instance, if a tape is missing I can use a program that shows if it's in the library, when it was last used and what drive it was used on.

Is it a typical first job?
I think so, because you really don't need any computer experience to get the job, but you can learn a lot at work and advance.

What kind of preparation did you have for it?
I took BASIC programming in high school and I had used PCs in college, but I didn't know anything about operating mainframes.

What was the hardest aspect at first of working in the field?
The hardest part for me has been the hours. I work from 6 P.M. to 6 A.M., and around 3 A.M. it gets pretty hard. Also, it's difficult to get used to sleeping during the day. Some people had trouble with the speed and accuracy part of the job. When you're pulling tapes from the vault or mounting them in the drives, you have to do it within a certain time frame.

How long did it take you to get established?
It took me about two weeks to feel comfortable at the job.

What do you like most about your work?
I work with some great people. They help me learn things besides the duties of this job so I'll be able to advance.

What do you like least?
It's kind of monotonous sometimes.

What has been your proudest achievement?
I'm proud that I'm a quick learner. I've only been at the job a few months, but because I can handle my own job and then some, I get some extra projects to do on the side. These extra tasks are very interesting and I like the challenges.

What advice would you offer someone who's thinking about entering this field?
You have to realize that you have to start at the bottom— but just look around and see all the areas that you can branch off into. A college degree might help you advance.

Debie Bridgham, 32,
computer operations manager,
Howard Johnson & Co.
Seattle, Washington
Years in the business: eight

How did you break into the field?
It's a funny story. After I graduated from high school in
Oregon, I bought a truck and moved to Los Angeles. I had
the truck financed by Wood Products Credit Union. Things
didn't work out for me in L.A., so I moved back to Oregon, and the credit union came to my home to repossess
the truck. When they met me, they decided I had spunk
and shortly afterward offered me a job as a teller. I worked
as a vault teller, but I indicated that I was interested in the
data processing field. After three years I was given the
opportunity to be a computer operator at the main branch.

What did you do on that job?
A credit union is similar to a bank. We used Chase Manhat-
tan Bank in New York as our clearinghouse. Each day, we
would open our computer system to allow Chase to transmit
drafts (checks) that our members had written. Then we
would try to post them, make a file of exceptions (nonsuffi-
cient funds, stop payments, etc.) and transfer that file back
to Chase at a specific time. We basically had the same
setup for other transmissions such as The Exchange (ATM)
and Visa.

My job was to make sure the batch jobs were running at
precisely the time necessary to receive files and transmit
back in the timeframe allowed. I processed tapes from
member companies that contained their employees' payroll
deductions for savings or loan payments. I had monthly
processes to do, including posting dividends, late notices,
certificate maturity notices and statement generation.

Was it a typical first job?
I don't think so, because of the way I got into it. I had my
foot in the door, which was unusual, and no educational
experience.

What was the hardest aspect of working in the field during your first few years?
Not having any computer science background. When you jump into the computer field, there are a lot of things that people assume you know. There were so many terms I was unfamiliar with; I didn't even know what bytes or mega-bytes were. So I bought the Time-Life series on computer basics and some other books, and read them at night so I could catch up. I also found people who knew a lot about computers and asked them a lot of questions.

How long did it take you to get established?
It probably took me a year to feel comfortable in my job because I had so much to learn.

What do you currently do?
The company I work for processes retirement fund and benefits information for 1,100 client firms. We receive payroll information (usually on magnetic tape) from the client. We determine the format of the tape (machine lan-guage, record size, etc.) and copy it onto our Hewlett-Packard machines. Our consultants work with that informa-tion and then involve operations again, generating statements for the client companies.

Statements are printed in house on line or laser printers, or a laser tape is created for printing off site by a service bureau.

I work in the data center of the company's corporate head-quarters, which serves eight offices around the nation. I manage the rotation and retention of tapes in the tape li-brary, oversee the printers and operate two minicomputers (Hewlett Packard 3000s) and the tape drives and printers that go with them. I process jobs for the clients when they ask for them. In the computer room we have personal com-puters that interface with our eight offices; the PCs control the network and their connections to our mainframes.

What do you like most about your work?
I really enjoy being in a supportive role and solving problems.

What do you like least?
That I'm so tied to my job. I get calls 24 hours a day be-

cause the computers are running around the clock. I can't remember the last night that I didn't get a call at home about a problem. When I was on vacation recently, I had to call in to see what was going on, and I got calls about problems.

What has been your proudest achievement?
I feel most proud about providing support, meeting deadlines and maintaining a good working relationship with our users.

What advice would you offer someone who's thinking about entering this field?
An associate degree would help someone who wants to enter the field. Everyone has different self-motivation, and I don't know if the struggle I went through to catch up on the industry would work for most people.

John Seymour, 49,
system control operator, Nordstrom, Seattle, Washington
Years in the business: 15

How did you break into the field?
I had one year of electronics training in the Navy, and when I got out, I decided I wanted to be a doctor. I went into college as a premed major and looked for a nightshift job so I could work my way through school. I didn't have any computer experience, but I heard that data processing was a good way to get night work, so I went to an employment agency. I got hired by Sun Oil as an entry-level operator; I loaded tapes into a tape drive, and I ripped apart printouts, put them in stacks and delivered them.

After a year of the premed program, I dropped out of school and moved to Santa Monica, California. I entered the city college to major in math and got a nightshift job as an operator at Atlantic Richfield.

What was the hardest aspect of working in the field during your first few years?
It was very confusing. I had no idea what was going on

inside the machines, and I had no idea what I was doing. My supervisors would leave me at night with this machine and tell me to turn this button on at this time, but I had no idea what that did.

How long did it take you to get established?
It took me three to four months to feel comfortable as a computer operator.

How many different jobs have you held in the field?
I've had three positions at Nordstrom and worked as an operator for three companies before that.

What do you currently do?
I'm a system control operator, working in systems operation and network operations. I keep an eye on the subsystems running on each machine, making sure they are not choked, locked up, backed up or taking up too much CPU (central processing unit memory). There are 30 to 40 subsystems in a machine at the same time. When a subsystem breaks, I do the first-level troubleshooting, then I call in the "owner" of the subsystem (a systems programmer) to fix it.

What do you like most about your work?
That I can be myself on the job. I can wear anything I want, say anything and do anything, as long as I get the work done and treat people right. It's a relaxed, free atmosphere, not stressful at all.

What do you like least?
Two things. First, every couple of days there's a new system, a new machine and new manuals, and I'm left in the middle of the night, not knowing what to do with them. Second, when something goes wrong, the responsibility for the problem often falls on the lowliest people—those of us in the computer room. The system can be down, the clock is ticking, we've got to fix it fast. Nobody else will believe or admit that their part of the configuration could be the problem.

What has been your proudest achievement?
Making shift supervisor. It was a goal of mine and I reached it.

What advice would you offer someone who's thinking about entering this field?
A lot of people don't know that mainframe computers need to be operated, but they do, and doing that work is a great way to get into the field. You don't need a college degree or experience; you just need a good attitude.

It used to be that when a company needed something printed—a brochure or business cards, manuals or reports—it had to hire several people: a professional typesetter, a designer and a printing firm. Today, that job can be prepared by one person with a personal computer, special page-composition software, a scanner and a laser printer. That person is often called a desktop publishing specialist.

D esktop publishing specialists can manipulate words and images into an interesting format—choosing the best type sizes and styles, boxes, rules, shapes and shading, and taking care of design, layout and formatting specifications. They might also select clipart (illustrations from a library on disk), create graphs or charts, or scan photographs or illustrations into the computer with a scanner. (A scanner is a device that reads images and text from printed pages and converts them to digital information that the computer software can understand and retranslate to images on the screen.) The final product, whether it's a newsletter, brochure or slide show, can be printed on a laser printer or other appropriate device or taken to a service bureau that has more sophisticated printers and output devices.

Electronic typesetting procedures were created in the 1970s, but it wasn't until 1984 that software was created for use on a personal computer. Because the job of desktop publishing specialist is a relatively new and evolving one, there are no hard and fast rules about what you need to be able to do beyond knowing how to use word processing, graphics and page layout software. A graphic design background is very useful, as is a good command of the English language.

The position of desktop publishing specialist itself sometimes defies categorization. The person who handles desktop publishing for a business or an organization may have another title—secretary, graphic designer or editor—and other job skills or responsibilities. But there are companies where the job of desktop publishing is one that consists primarily of formatting text and graphic elements into a finished product.

Some desktop publishing specialists work in corporations that have a regular need to create polished printed and/or graphic materials. They may work in the word processing, art, corporate training, corporate communications or public and investor relations departments. Others put their know-how to use in copy shops that offer desktop publishing services to corporate and individual clients.

If you enjoy working on computers and have a sense of design, desktop publishing may be the right niche for you.

What You Need to Know

- ❏ Basics of page layout and design
- ❏ Typography terms and codes
- ❏ Basics of print production

Necessary Skills

- ❏ Use one or more desktop publishing software programs
- ❏ Work easily with at least one program in each of the following categories: word processing, graphics and database management (arranging and accessing information in list form)
- ❏ Attention to detail
- ❏ Good listening and verbal skills (you will need to ask questions to make sure you produce what the creator of the document wants)

Do You Have What It Takes?

- ❏ Ability to be calm and productive under pressure of deadlines
- ❏ Diplomacy (you may have to explain why something cannot be done or had to be done differently without ruffling the feathers of people you work for or with)
- ❏ Interest in regularly updating your software skills
- ❏ The vision to conceptualize what the final product should look like
- ❏ Good eye-hand coordination and manual dexterity (using a mouse to draw, rule or perform other desktop publishing functions requires a steady hand)

Education

A high school diploma is recommended. Computer skills, however they have been acquired, are a must. Design, layout, typography and production coursework is highly recommended.

Licenses Required

None

Job Outlook ◆ **Competition for jobs:** somewhat competitive

Producing materials in house is a money-saver for companies. Even though more employers will bring desktop publishing in house for that reason, competition for jobs is likely to be tough because a number of people already on staff (particularly secretaries and designers) have software skills and can learn desktop publishing. Still, there is and will continue to be a marketplace for competent desktop publishing specialists.

The Ground Floor ◆ *Entry-Level Jobs*

The specific responsibilities of the people who have any of the following job titles varies, but all involve working on a computer to combine text and graphic elements.

❑ Desktop publishing operator
❑ Desktop publishing specialist
❑ Electronic publishing specialist
❑ Publications specialist

On-the-Job Responsibilities ◆ *Beginners and Experienced Desktop Publishing Specialists*

❑ Complete projects according to client or document creator's guidelines
❑ Make sure all parts of the project are turned in on schedule for printing and distribution
❑ Mock up several layouts to be evaluated
❑ Select potential typefaces (client or creator may or may not want final say)
❑ Determine which images from clipart collections are most appropriate
❑ Scan illustrations or photographs (into the software)
❑ Print out final approved version or arrange for the disk to be printed out at a service bureau

If you work for a company whose hours are nine to five, your schedule will be the same. If, however, people are late in supplying you with copy and art, you may have to work extra hours or through lunch to make sure the job is done on time. If you work for a copy shop, you may be expected to work some evening and weekend hours in addition to regular daytime hours. There are good possibilities for part-time work with copy shops, and even work from home possibilities, provided you have all the necessary equipment.

When You'll Work

Corporate desktop publishing specialists get the same vacation and holiday as other employees. That generally means all major national holidays off, one week of vacation after the first year of work, and two after the second year. Paid vacation time is not always as uniform at copy shops.

Time Off

❑ Publishing companies—small newspapers, magazines, textbook and newsletter publishing specialists
❑ Public relations and advertising firms
❑ Copy shops (independently owned, franchises and chains)
❑ Service bureaus (they perform many of the same functions as copy shops but usually have personal computers available for use by clients as well)

Who's Hiring

Any large organization that has personal computers and the need to create polished, professional-looking printed materials, including:
❑ Banks, insurance companies and financial services companies
❑ Universities and school systems

❑ Carpal tunnel syndrome (a wrist fatigue injury caused by constant keyboarding)
❑ Eye strain and headaches (from looking at a computer screen for hours at a time)
❑ Back and shoulder strain (if your chair, desk height and monitor position are not adjusted properly)

On-the-Job Hazards

Places You'll Go

Beginners and experienced desktop publishing specialists: no potential for travel.

Anything created on the computer can be telecommunicated or sent using more conventional delivery modes.

Surroundings

Desktop publishing specialists either work in officelike environments (which can range from simple to elegant) or in the storefront environments of copy shops or service bureaus.

Dollars and Cents

Starting salary: $18,000 to $22,000
After 5 years: $28,000 to $38,000
Top earners: $50,000 +

Moving Up

In this new job area there is no defined career path. Whether or how you advance depends a great deal on the skills you have beyond knowing how to run desktop publishing software. Strong design and editorial skills can help you carve yourself an important niche in the corporate world. Or, if you demonstrate the ability to train and direct the work of others, you may be able to move into a supervisory position.

Another possibility is to set up your own desktop publishing business. To make that a reality, you will need to be accomplished at meeting deadlines, have a good head for business and have the ability to coordinate and direct the work of others whom you may hire or contract work with. Of course, you'll also need to have state-of-the-art equipment of your own and at least one or two clients to start.

Where the Jobs Are

Jobs are concentrated in major metropolitan areas where there are large companies, publishing specialists, advertising and public relations firms and copy shops that service corporate clients.

Schooling

Courses in desktop publishing and design are offered by community colleges, technical and art schools, adult education centers and through the adult education divisions of some high schools. Copy shops and service bureaus sometimes offer individual or small group instruction in desktop publishing software.

Desktop publishing attracts both men and women since it combines graphic design with computer skills.

◆ **The Male/Female Equation**

The Bad News

❏ Having to execute the vision of someone whose design skills are negligible or nonexistent
❏ Working under deadline pressure
❏ Having to please people who may not appreciate what can and cannot be done easily
❏ The pressure of juggling more than one project

The Good News

❏ Opportunity to share your ideas and artistic vision
❏ Part-time work options
❏ Opportunity to use computer and design skills
❏ Exposure for your own finished product

◆ **Making Your Decision: What to Consider**

National Association of Desktop Publishing Specialists
462 Old Boston Street, Suite 8
Topsfield, Massachusetts 01983
617-887-7900

◆ **More Information Please**

For $95 a year, members receive a newsletter and magazine each month and can get discounts on desktop publishing books and manuals.

The Newsletter Clearinghouse
P.O. Box 311
Rhinebeck, New York 12572
914-876-2081

The company publishes "Newsletter Design," a publication that reviews newsletters, suggesting ways to improve them ($125 a year), and "The Newsletter on Newsletters," which provides tips and information on all aspects of desktop publishing ($120 a year).

Newsletter Publishing Specialists Association
1401 Wilson Blvd. #207
Arlington, Virginia 22209
703-527-2333

A not-for-profit trade association, this group provides information on publishing newsletters as a for-profit business. Because it is geared for money-making enterprises, the cost of membership is high: $375 a year. The association provides information on all levels of production, from graphic design to printing. The "Hot Line" newsletter goes out to members every other week, along with instructional publications and information about conferences and workshops.

Scott Piteo, 29,
electronic forms operator,
SAFECO Insurance,
Seattle, Washington
Years in the business: seven

How did you break into the field?
In high school I did some part-time layout work, and I studied art and art history in college. But it's hard to support yourself as an artist, so I got a job as a delivery person with a typography and printing shop. When one of the typesetters quit, I was offered the job, and I learned about typesetting. But after a few years the company was losing a lot of business to service bureaus who print work that people prepare on their own computers. I had to get a new job.

My second job was pretty much the same except that they used Macintoshes there instead of dedicated typesetting equipment. But they were having financial trouble, too, and after about six months I started looking for another job. I saw an ad for a desktop publishing spot at SAFECO Insurance and started there in July 1991.

What does your job entail?
I started out doing forms. The company has about 20,000 different insurance forms that were prepared on an old in-house publishing system, and they wanted to convert them all to a new desktop publishing system. Using a Sun work-station and a mouse, I recreated the forms exactly as they looked before. It was a very typical first job.

Now I'm doing other work besides the forms. We got a couple of Macintoshes in the department last September, so now I'm using *PageMaker* to do a lot of promotional pieces, such as brochures with information about insurance or mutual funds.

What was the hardest aspect of the work in the beginning?
I had no benefits or job security at the small typesetting companies. At SAFECO the toughest part was the routine of all those forms.

How long did it take you to get established?
At my first job, it took about four months to get comfort-able with the computer and the typesetting work. At SAFECO, it only took about a week because I started on the Sun systems, which were a lot like the Macintoshes I had been using.

What do you like most about your work?
The creative aspect. I'm doing more work that has more graphics, so I use a scanner and a program called *Adobe Photo Shop.*

What do you like least?
When people come to us for jobs, they sometimes don't understand what desktop publishing really entails, and they are overwhelmed by all of the options. They can't make decisions about what they want; they keep having us do the job different ways, with different type sizes and styles, and it seems they don't know where to end.

What has been your proudest achievement?
Last December the chief executive officer of SAFECO retired, and he was honored in early May by the City of Hope at a gala ball. I put together a 40-page, four-color journal for the event, with photos of the CEO as a kid,

captions, statements and photos from Washington government officials, and advertisements. Managers of the company have told me how good it turned out and that people at the ball were commenting favorably about it.

What advice would you offer someone who's thinking about entering this field?
Find a job with a company that is trying to stay on the cutting edge of the technology. Things change so fast in this field—they've changed a lot just since I started a year ago—and if you don't keep up, someone who is will push you aside.

Carolyn Kietzke, 48, administrative support, Bear Creek Country Club, Woodinville, Washington
Years in the business: two

How did you break into the field?
I went from high school to marriage and motherhood. I didn't work outside the home for 25 years, until my youngest daughter graduated from high school. My first job was working as a clerk in a fabric store, but after four years I was burned out. I got tired of dealing with the public, and I had to work some nights, weekends and holidays.

About the time I started wondering what else I could do, I got a flyer in the mail from a local vocational tech school. The computer courses looked interesting, although I had never touched a computer. You didn't need experience for the class, you only needed to be able to type. So for six months I was a full-time student in a business computers training program. We worked on both PCs and Macintoshes, and learned *Lotus* and *Excel* (a database program), *WordPerfect, Microsoft Word* and *PageMaker*. I liked *PageMaker* best—it's a precise kind of thing. Someone told me I like that because I'm detail oriented.

When the program was over, I saw an ad in the paper for a secretary/receptionist familiar with *PageMaker*, and I thought, Bingo! I applied for the job, which is at a country club, and found they wanted someone to start producing their newsletter in house.

How long did it take you to get established?
It took maybe four months before I felt comfortable with what I was doing.

What do you currently do?
I answer phones, direct calls and do administrative work for four department heads and the country club's general manager. I also produce the club's monthly newsletter, as well as calendars for golf programs, menus for the Players' Lounge and flyers for special events such as tournaments and luncheons—all with the *PageMaker*.

What do you like most about your work?
I love working with computers. I'm so fascinated with learning about the programs and figuring out better ways to use the software. With desktop publishing, I like the process of starting with a few pages of written information and figuring out the best way to convey the message with different fonts and graphics.

What do you like least?
Sometimes the limitations of the software can be frustrating. For example, when I wanted to use larger type sizes, I had to create them on the computer, use the copy machine to enlarge them and then paste them on the page. I tried to use a printer attachment and a *PostScript* emulator for this, but neither worked very well. Then recently we got the newest upgrade for *Windows*, and it has true type fonts, scalable up to 72 points, and a nice variety.

What has been your proudest achievement?
I'm very proud of the work I've done on the newsletter. I know I'm saving the club a lot of money by doing it in house, and I've also been getting a lot of compliments about it from the club members. I'm proud when it goes out to members on time with the correct information.

What advice would you offer someone who's thinking about entering this field?
Spend the time to take a computer business training course. It opens so many doors for you. Most want ads you see

are not just for secretaries and receptionists but for people who have computer experience as well, especially with *PageMaker, WordPerfect* and *Lotus.*

Avonne Beaver, 34,
art director and production manager,
AlphaGraphics,
Charleston, South Carolina
Years in the business: five

How did you break into the field?
Both of my brothers are artists and they have their own sign companies, and when I was growing up I was always being compared to them. So I went the opposite direction and started working as a tax consultant in Charlotte, North Carolina. When my husband and I moved to Charleston, I decided to go to a technical college to get an associate degree in industrial design. I got a minor in commercial graphics. In my second year of school I participated in a co-op program with DuPont that allowed students with certain grade point averages to work part time while in school. After I finished the program, I stayed on with DuPont in computer graphics for another year.

What did you do on your first job?
I started at DuPont doing slide show presentations and graphics that would appear on monitors throughout the plant to show to visitors as they walked through. But I did my work on an IBM mainframe, so my first real desktop publishing job wasn't until I went to AlphaGraphics two years ago.

Was your DuPont position a typical first job?
I think it's typical if you have some design and computer experience like I did.

What kind of preparation did you have for it?
I had worked a little on computers, and I had the technical degree.

What was the hardest aspect of working in the field during your first few years?

45

It was hard at first to find a happy medium between the customers' needs—they always need the work done yesterday—and meeting those deadlines. It's a balancing act.

How long did it take you to get established?
It took me a full year to feel established because I had to learn all the different software. It is a constant challenge because we keep upgrading the software we have.

What do you currently do?
I design monthly and quarterly newsletters on a regular basis for customers, and I design brochures, logos, business cards, letterhead, advertisements and posters for clients who come to AlphaGraphics. They consult with me about what they want, and I walk them through their options and give them advice. I have a scanner so I can scan text in, but for some clients we type it in.

What do you like most about your work?
I like getting to see things I've created out in public. It's a great feeling to open a newspaper and see an advertisement I have made.

What do you like least?
What makes it difficult is some customers' lack of knowledge as to what this industry is all about. It's hard to handle that very diplomatically.

What has been your proudest achievement?
Last fall I had the opportunity to work with MGM when the movie company was in town to work on a film (*Rich In Love*). At the last minute they wanted to add beer bottles in a scene, and they didn't have time to get permission from one of the beer companies to use their logo. So the props manager came in and showed me a sample of what he wanted. I created a label that he liked and made a thousand copies of it. He used it for the film and said he would use the rest of the logos I made in other films that have beer-drinking scenes.

What advice would you offer someone who's thinking about entering this field?
At this point I think it might be hard to get into the field without some kind of design school training. You need

some computer knowledge, so you should make sure the design school you choose offers computer experience. Some people may think that desktop publishing means you're just sitting there typing, but a lot of creativity goes into it.

You're surrounded by the latest technology; monitors with stunning graphics, state-of-the-art laptops, brightly packaged software programs. The customer walks into the store. Now it's up to you. It might be as simple as locating the right cable, or you might have to help him or her set up the perfect PC system. Fewer feelings are sweeter for the computer salesperson than making the sale and—making the customer's day.

Some 45 million personal computers are in use in the U.S., 10 percent of which are in households. While big corporations generally buy their equipment directly from manufacturers' representatives, home users and small-business owners usually turn to retail outlets and direct sales vendors (companies who telemarket their equipment) for their computer purchases. These customers depend on local salespeople to help determine what equipment is best for them, to demonstrate different models and software and to build a system that serves their needs.

Computer salespeople generally work in retail stores, in the computer departments of department or discount stores or in the newly emerging superstores that carry everything a computer user needs. Employers look for applicants who like computers and are familiar with how they work, who are energetic and personable and who have the patience to guide consumers in their purchases. If you love talking about computers and what they can do, you may be a good candidate for retail computer sales.

A computer salesperson has a big responsibility: for many buyers, purchasing a system can be a big-ticket item and critical to the smooth running of their businesses. As a salesperson you need to listen carefully to what the customers' needs are and what they are willing to spend. Your recommendation of the right equipment not only insures future business with that customer but also the referrals they generate.

And just think: you'll be able to hack around with the newest, state-of-the-art hardware and software—and get paid for having fun!

What You Need to Know

❑ The basic functions and components of computer systems

❑ In-depth knowledge of the types of computers your store specializes in

❑ Ability to load, bring up and execute commands of popular word processing, spreadsheet and graphics programs (used to demonstrate capabilities of particular computer systems)

❑ History of the computer models and systems you're selling

Necessary Skills

❑ Good math skills (so you can speak knowledgeably about computer memory and speed)

❑ Familiarity with calculators

❑ Salesmanship, gift of gab

❑ Aptitude for explaining and demonstrating products to customers

Do You Have What It Takes?

❑ A friendly, outgoing personality

❑ A well-groomed appearance

❑ The power of persuasion

❑ Ability to maintain your cool when customers become difficult or rude

❑ A positive attitude that allows you to shrug off rejection

❑ Strong legs—you'll often be on your feet most of the day

❑ A good telephone manner

❑ Discipline to organize your workday

❑ Ability to negotiate and make compromises so that you can close a deal

Education

A high school education is recommended. Some computer training or coursework is very helpful. Once you are hired, you may be given on-the-job training or be sent to training courses (several days to several weeks in length) offered by your employer.

Licenses Required

None

Job Outlook

Job openings will grow: faster than average
Sales of computers are expected to continue growing, which creates a rosy outlook for those interested in sales. Although computer sales jobs may take different forms as the types of outlets at which users purchase equipment evolve (i.e., superstores and direct vendor sales), landing a position in sales should not be difficult for those with a good knowledge of PCs and strong sales skills.

The Ground Floor

Entry-level jobs: sales trainee, floor salesperson

On-the-Job Responsibilities

Beginners

❑ Greet walk-in customers and determine their needs
❑ Demonstrate products—hardware and software
❑ Locate the correct cables and accessories requested by customers
❑ Ring up sales at the cash register
❑ Help stock shelves and do inventory control

Experienced Salespeople

All of the above, plus:
❑ Explain the technical aspects of various hardware and software and the advantages of each
❑ Make recommendations about how to expand current systems, which computer or component would complement the customer's current equipment and when to invest in a new system

- Give technical advice about simple computer problems experienced by customers
- Make referrals to the computer service department or to individual technicians
- Deal with corporate clients who come to the store (sometimes)
- May work with manufacturers' representatives who want their products sold in the store
- Train new members of the sales staff
- Negotiate deals for large ticket-price components or system (subject to approval by manager)
- Explain store or manufacturer's warranties and financing options
- Meet sales goals (set by the sales manager on a weekly, monthly or quarterly basis)

When You'll Work

Retail sales jobs involve long hours (45 to 50 hours a week is typical). Stores are open when people can shop, which generally includes evening hours, weekends and some holidays. In a store that is open both Saturday and Sunday, salespeople usually work one of the two. Options for part-time work are good.

Time Off

Some major holidays are big shopping days, and if the store is open, you may have to work. Generally, sales employees get one week of vacation after their first year of service, two weeks after their second.

Perks

- Discounts on hardware and software carried by the store

Who's Hiring

- Retail computer stores, including independently owned stores, franchises and chain stores
- Department and discount stores that sell computers
- Superstores (some specialize in computer products only; others sell all kinds of office products)
- Local vendors (they specialize in IBM-compatible clones and assemble generic systems on site, using

components from a variety of sources)

Telemarketing sales representatives

❑ Mailorder firms (they sell a variety of products from different manufacturers)
❑ Direct sales vendors (they manufacture and sell their own brand; some provide after-sale support, including on-site service and extended warranties)

Places You'll Go

Beginners or experienced salespeople: little travel potential.

Those who work for a chain may be sent to another city or location for additional training or seminars. Traveling to the regional office of a computer manufacturer to attend informational sessions when new models are introduced is another possibility.

Surroundings

Like other retail operations, computer stores are pleasant working environments, that is, if you don't mind not having a space of your own and being around customers all the time. Most stores have large windows and their share of sunlight unless they're in a mall. Superstores often have more of a warehouse environment, while smaller stores are more like small offices with their set-ups of various computer systems for customers to try out. Busiest times are at lunch, after five and on weekends.

Dollars and Cents

Beginners: $18,000 to $24,000
With five years' experience: $30,000 to $45,000
Top experienced salespeople: $40,000 to $70,000
Some computer salespeople work on a straight hourly or salary basis; most work on a salary plus commission basis. If you are good at what you do, you'll make more if you work on a commission basis.

Sales trainees generally earn $1,000 to $1,200 a month base salary plus a commission on any sales they make. After three to six months, the commissions they earn (which are likely to be more substantial) are a draw against the salary they earn (in other words, their base salary is in effect an advance against future commissions). Commissions range from 8 to 20 percent of gross sales. Some stores pay each salesperson their share of the pool (the total commissions earned by all store salespeople). Bonuses may be given for exceptional sales or as an incentive when a store is having a particularly good year.

Sales representatives can move up to being sales leads (head sales people). Those who demonstrate they not only know how to sell but also how to train and motivate others and keep track of store operations—inventory, display and accounting—can move up to sales supervisor or assistant store manager. Once you show that you are capable of heading up a team of salespeople or running the store in the manager's absence, you may be promoted to store manager. The next steps up—regional or district sales or store manager—are sometimes awarded to those with a good track record, but some national store chains look for a two- or even four-year business degree before they promote someone to manager.

Moving Up

Opportunities in retail computer sales are available all across the country. Most shopping malls and central business districts contain at least one computer or office products store; major metropolitan areas have hundreds and are increasingly sprouting superstores.

Where the Jobs Are

Coursework in business and computer subjects can make you a more attractive applicant for a computer sales job and a more successful salesperson. In particular, check into courses in marketing, sales, merchandising and business administration. The more computer operating systems you're familiar with and the more software applications you can comfortably use, the better. Both computer and business courses are offered through the adult education

School Information

divisions of high schools, community colleges and four-year colleges, among other places.

Men dominate retail computer sales, although an increasing number of women are entering the field.

The Male/Female Equation

Making Your Decision: What to Consider

The Bad News	*The Good News*
❑ Paycheck varies depending on your sales	❑ Potential to make high salary if sales are good
❑ Evening and weekend work	❑ Opportunities to buy equipment at discount prices
❑ Job insecurity; business goes through growth and shrinkage cycles	❑ First to see new products and innovations
❑ Stress of dealing with difficult customers	❑ Get paid to talk about computers
❑ Have very little "down time"	❑ Time flies quickly on busy days

WHAT IT'S REALLY LIKE

Jon Nitto, 20,
sales representative, Computerland Express,
Atlanta, Georgia
Years in the business: one

How did you break into the field?
My father used to work in a computer store in upstate New
York. He told me about the opening and I applied for it.
Since I worked in his store when I was young and had two
years' retail experience at a clothing store, I got the job.

What do you do?
I'm responsible mostly for sales; my main duty is helping
customers. I also do some stocking work, merchandising
and answering phone calls about prices and product avail-
ability. We don't work on commission, but our supervisors
do keep track of our sales, so I'll write up the quote sheet
(a bill with items sold and at what price) and my number
gets entered at the register. I'm in transition because I just
got a promotion; I'll soon be in charge of a new department
that deals only in Macintosh computers.

What's been the hardest aspect of the job so far?
It's hard to maintain product knowledge when things change so much and so quickly. We get new models every six months, and it's next to impossible to try to keep up with the software.

How long did it take you to feel established?
We had a couple of weeks of training at Computerland University before the store opened, and that helped a lot. Even so, it was unsettling during grand opening weekend when we had 7,000 people come through the store. It took me about two months before I felt comfortable in the job.

What do you like most about your work?
It's exciting to see the new products, to know what's coming out before the customers do.

What do you like least?
Retail sales can be exhausting. You always have to be a chipper person, and I'm not always feeling so chipper. And I hate feeling like a fake. But that's just how retailing is.

What has been your proudest achievement?
My promotion. It's nice to be appreciated and to have people realize you're doing your job.

What advice would you offer someone who's thinking about entering this field?
If you decide on retail sales instead of corporate sales, go with a big established company. I'm not sure those Mom and Pop computer stores will be around for long. Maybe they can offer more individual service than larger stores can, but right now customers want price, price, price—and the smaller stores can't have prices that are as low.

Mike Spear, 26,
sales lead, Ballard Computer,
Seattle, Washington
Years in the business: three

How did you break into the field?
I was stationed in the Seattle area when I was in the military, and I really liked it. After I got out, my wife and I

moved from Iowa to Seattle. She's a nurse, so we knew she could find a job. I saw a Help Wanted sign in a Radio Shack window, walked in and applied. I didn't have any experience in computers, electronics or sales, but I'd been using an IBM XT at home and I'd taken a college-level programming course. I got the job and started at $5 an hour, selling everything from antennas and stereos to computers.

Was that a typical first job?
Yes. I wasn't making much money, but I got a lot of experience almost immediately. I was learning how to sell, learning about electronics products. It was very intense. In a small retail store like that, where there are only four or five salespeople, you do everything—you help with inventory, restock shelves, answer phones, do closing and security procedures and make deposits.

Five months after being hired I was manager of the store. I was 24 years old. You can read all the books you want—and that's important—but you need hands-on experience. On the sales floor you have to perform on the machines.

What was the hardest aspect of working in the field in the beginning?
Everything I had to learn. The sales process was completely foreign to me. You actually have to follow steps in a sales cycle, and I learned most of that on the floor.

How long did it take you to get established?
Sales positions have an amazing amount of turnover, so you can earn seniority very quickly. I feel comfortable when I have seniority over a few people, and that happened in just a few months.

How many different jobs have you held in this field?
Seven jobs with two companies. I started in sales at a Radio Shack electronics store, was a management trainee at a different Radio Shack store and then was manager of another store. After that I was a salesperson at a Tandy/Radio Shack business center, then manager of one of the business centers. I started at Ballard as a salesperson, and now I'm a sales lead.

What do you currently do?

I back up the floor manager. When he's unavailable, I handle customer issues. I deal with customers who are unhappy with their service or who need to exchange something. But my main responsibility is selling. I don't do any inventory or restocking, which is unique at this store.

What do you like most about your work?

This is an extremely fun place to work. You have to enjoy what you're doing or it becomes too much of an effort to come in to work.

What do you like least?

I hate closing the store because it means working late at night. I'm a morning person, and until recently I had to be here sometimes until 10 P.M., and then I had an hour commute home. In retail sales it's never a nine to five job. You have to be open when the customers are going to buy.

What has been your proudest achievement?

I've never been in a position where I haven't been promoted almost immediately, sometimes ahead of peers who started before me. I like being in charge.

What advice would you offer someone who's thinking about entering this field?

Get hands-on experience any way you can. And a caution: if you're a shy person, this is not the place for you to be.

Craig Simpson, 39,
district manager, Egghead Software,
Seattle, Washington
Years in the business: eight

How did you break into the field?

I bought a computer in late 1984 because I was looking for a job. I heard that Egghead was a good place to buy software, and when I went to the store, I saw a Help Wanted sign. They were looking for a salesperson and also an assistant manager. I applied to be the assistant manager; it paid more. I had retail experience at a sporting goods store, and I'd also worked for a broadcast properties broker where

I had used an IBM PC to do word processing, spreadsheet and database work. I was hired.

What did your job involve?
I was responsible for sales on the floor, for working with customers, ordering product, inventory controls, cash controls and general housekeeping.

Was it a typical first job?
No, because at the time, Egghead was a new commodity. Before it started, the main place people bought software was from computer hardware vendors. Then Egghead started selling software below their prices. I think that because Egghead was a discounter we had to work harder to prove that having low prices didn't mean we didn't know about the product.

What was the hardest aspect of working in the field during your first few years?
Sometimes I'd spend an hour providing customer service over the phone, helping someone use a program, while I had people waiting in the store for help. That was a challenge. Another was learning new core programs. The hard part is knowing what you don't know and when to get help. When I didn't know how to do something with a program I'd call the manufacturer or ask someone I worked with.

How many different jobs have you held in the field?
I've had three positions at six Egghead stores. I started as assistant manager of the Bellevue store, then was transferred to our South Center mall store to do the same job. Six months later I became manager of that store. I helped open one store and then managed the downtown Seattle store. Now I'm the district manager for the state of Washington.

What does your job entail?
I'm responsible for hiring managers, assistant managers and salespeople in all of the stores in the region. I make sure stores run according to operational procedures. I also train managers and look for sites for expansion.

What do you like most about your work?
I like to find out about customers—what they use the computer for and how they use it. I like to satisfy their needs and then discover needs they didn't know they had.

What do you like least?

When customers have a problem, they sometimes forget that the person on the other side of the counter is a human being. Customers can be angry or belligerent sometimes, even when the problem isn't with our software or service.

What has been your proudest achievement?

I'm proud that in my years with Egghead, I've made contributions to the company and what I've said has been heard. I have influence.

What advice would you offer someone who's thinking about entering this field?

Don't go into retail unless you like people. You really need to enjoy being around them.

Telephone lines used to transmit only voices; now, fiber-optic cables are used to transmit computerized data so that people in distant places can exchange information the length of a book in a matter of minutes. The specialists who install and service networks—as small as ten people or as large as thousands of computer users—are tele-communications technicians.

While telecommunications technicians include people who install and repair telephone lines, the information in this chapter refers primarily to those technicians who specialize in data communications.

Employment prospects for those who service telephones are expected to decline because of enormous productivity increases associated with the computerization of telecommunications equipment.

The job outlook for technicians who specialize in data communications, on the other hand, is promising because the same companies that installed computers in the eighties now want to link them together so that users can easily access information. Companies that have more than 250 computers often hire technicians to join their staffs; smaller businesses often hire third-party maintenance organizations that employ technicians to install and maintain their networks for them.

Technicians set up the cables, modems, computers and telecommunications software so that different types of computers can talk to each other or communicate with a central source. And when computer users experience a problem using the network, technicians track down the source of the problem and take care of it. As much as one-fifth of a technician's time, however, may be spent on administrative types of tasks.

If you are a tinkerer, the kind of person who has always enjoyed taking things apart to figure out how they work, and if you are a fan of computers, you will probably enjoy working as a telecommunications technician.

What You Need to Know

❏ Basic understanding of computer operating systems (*DOS, System Files, OS-2*); hardware (IBM and IBM compatibles, Apple and Hewlett-Packard peripherals); software (word processing, spreadsheet, database and telecommunications)

❏ Basic concepts of telecommunications

❏ Basic concepts of analog and digital switching systems

❏ Digital applications of LANs (not a requirement but a big plus)

❏ Relationships between voltage, current and resistance and how they are measured

Necessary Skills

❏ How to connect computers, modems and phone lines

❏ How to install software on different types of computers

❏ Facility with tools such as screwdrivers

❏ Good listening and verbal skills (you need to pay close attention to the problem as described by a customer and ask good questions)

❏ Strong reading and comprehension skills (equipment is changing constantly, and you have to read and refer to manuals to keep up to date)

Do You Have What It Takes?

❏ Patience, persistence (locating the source of a problem isn't always easy)

❏ Problem-solving ability to troubleshoot why something isn't working

❏ Physical strength (you must sometimes pick up equipment that may weigh up to 80 pounds)

❏ Tolerance for dealing with people who are irate, frustrated or unhappy because their computers are not working

❏ A soothing disposition (be reassuring and cool as a

◆ **Getting into the Field**

cucumber in dealing with users in distress)

Education

No education beyond high school is required, although coursework in computers and telecommunications is helpful. In particular, courses on digital topics, programming (to develop analytical thinking skills), hardware, operating systems and software are recommended.

Licenses Required

None. Some manufacturers, however, offer what's called product certification, which indicates that you know how to work with particular types of networks; but earning this certification does not necessarily make you more attractive to an employer.

Job Outlook

Competition for jobs: some competition

As more businesses decide to set up LANs or hook into WANs (wide-area networks), there will be an increasing need for technicians who can install, monitor and maintain these networks.

The Ground Floor

Entry-level job: telecommunications technician

On-the-Job Responsibilities

Beginners

❑ Configure computer equipment and install telecommunications programs
❑ Connect telephone cables to phone, computers, modems and fax/modem cards and standalones
❑ Provide support to network users (solve problems on the phone or make an appearance and fix them)
❑ Check for network problems involving computer and communications hardware and software as well as transmission facilities

❏ Perform repairs on modems, fax/modems and other telecommunications peripherals

❏ Order new parts, back up and ship back deficient parts

❏ Log all action taken, make copies and send to appropriate parties

❏ Enter information about the end user, problem and solution into databases (clients and management often want to know everything that's done to help them make judgments about updating equipment or about training)

Experienced Technicians

All of the above, plus:

❏ May tie two or more systems together into a network

❏ Troubleshoot network operations

❏ Supervise the work of less experienced technicians

When You'll Work

Technicians who work for end users who keep typical office hours often keep the same hours themselves. They may, however, also work after hours or on weekends or holidays when installing new equipment, doing routine maintenance or upgrading the network.

Technicians who work for companies that require round-the-clock network monitoring must sometimes work or be on call late at night (3 P.M. to 11 P.M.). Working an overnight shift (11 P.M. to 7 A.M.) is unusual, but if you work it, you are usually paid at a higher rate or can elect to get comp time (extra time off). Newcomers are most likely to get stuck with undesirable hours. Part-time work options are rare.

Time Off

Vacation, paid holidays and sick days depend on the type of employer. Technicians who are employed by large companies generally receive the same vacation allowances as other employees, which tend to be more generous than those of small businesses, such as retail stores and third-party maintenance organizations.

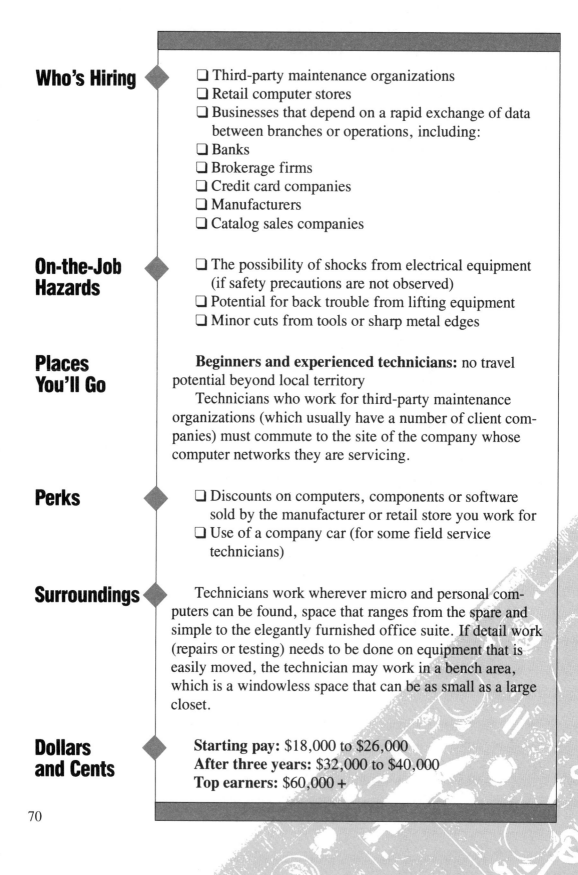

Who's Hiring

❏ Third-party maintenance organizations
❏ Retail computer stores
❏ Businesses that depend on a rapid exchange of data between branches or operations, including:
❏ Banks
❏ Brokerage firms
❏ Credit card companies
❏ Manufacturers
❏ Catalog sales companies

On-the-Job Hazards

❏ The possibility of shocks from electrical equipment (if safety precautions are not observed)
❏ Potential for back trouble from lifting equipment
❏ Minor cuts from tools or sharp metal edges

Places You'll Go

Beginners and experienced technicians: no travel potential beyond local territory

Technicians who work for third-party maintenance organizations (which usually have a number of client companies) must commute to the site of the company whose computer networks they are servicing.

Perks

❏ Discounts on computers, components or software sold by the manufacturer or retail store you work for
❏ Use of a company car (for some field service technicians)

Surroundings

Technicians work wherever micro and personal computers can be found, space that ranges from the spare and simple to the elegantly furnished office suite. If detail work (repairs or testing) needs to be done on equipment that is easily moved, the technician may work in a bench area, which is a windowless space that can be as small as a large closet.

Dollars and Cents

Starting pay: $18,000 to $26,000
After three years: $32,000 to $40,000
Top earners: $60,000 +

Highly ambitious technicians can almost double their earnings within a few years on the job if they acquire network expertise beyond doing the specific job tasks they are responsible for.

In order to move out of the role of technician and into a position as a telecommunications analyst or specialist, you need a complete understanding of how the network operates, including the hardware, software and operating system. A willingness to learn about new equipment is also critical since modifications and innovations happen so frequently. Your best chance for moving up is within a company whose network you have been servicing, because each network is somewhat unique. The job of the specialist or analyst is to monitor and maintain a company's communications network operations. You may have to give direction to technicians, which would require supervisory skills. And you may also get involved in telecommunications planning—the evaluation, selection and implementation of telecommunications software and hardware and other peripherals to upgrade the network.

◆ **Moving Up**

Jobs can be found wherever there are companies using computers. More opportunities are concentrated in major metropolitan areas, where the big users of computers and computer networking and third-party service bureaus are located.

◆ **Where the Jobs Are**

Courses and programs in computer technology and telecommunications are offered by a variety of places, including community colleges, post-high school vocational and technical schools, the adult education division of high schools and continuing education divisions of four-year colleges and universities.

◆ **Education Information**

The telecommunications field is still heavily dominated by men, but some recruiters note that more women are entering the field.

◆ **The Male/Female Equation**

Making Your Decision: What to Consider

The Bad News

❏ Plenty of paperwork
❏ Hassle of working with upset computer users
❏ Pressure to resolve problems quickly
❏ Benchwork can be tedious

The Good News

❏ Chance to earn good money
❏ Not being confined to any one work environment
❏ Good chance of promotion for the ambitious
❏ Opportunity to work on the cutting edge of an exciting field

More Information Please

IEEE Communications Society
c/o Institute of Electrical and Electronics Engineers
345 E. 47th Street
New York, New York 10017
212-705-7018

Telecommunications technicians and engineers may join the Communications Society alone for $47 a year or in conjunction with membership in IEEE ($15 plus the $95 IEEE fee).

North American Telecommunications Association
2000 M Street N.W., Suite 550
Washington, DC 20036
202-296-9800

Individuals join NATA through their employers, and membership fees are based on that company's sales. The association is geared to firms that manufacture and sell communications equipment and services.

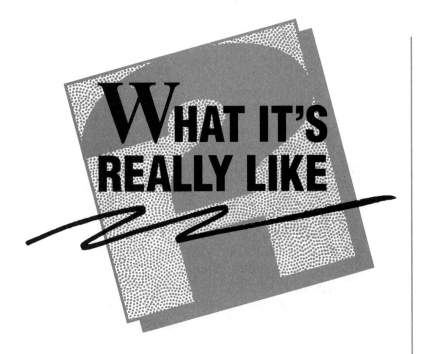

Thomas Carbone, 24,
communications tech I, Dow Jones & Co.,
Jersey City, New Jersey
Years in the business: five

How did you break into the field?

A friend who worked at Dow Jones got me a job in the
customer service department, taking all the trouble calls
from customers in the field when their equipment went
down. I wanted to get into field service, so I took a technical course at night. Some people in the class were in-house
technicians for Dow Jones, and they told me they would let
me know when there was an opening in the department.
When there was, they got me an interview with the department head.

What did you do on your first job?

In customer service I took the trouble calls and had to determine if the problems were with the equipment or telephone
lines. Then I'd let the dispatcher know, and he would dis-
patch a tech to go out to the customer. After two years in

customer service I became a field service dispatcher and did that for one and a half years.

Was it a typical first job?
Yes. It was a good way to get a foot in the door at Dow Jones, and I learned a lot. In my second job, when I became a field service dispatcher, I got to go out on some field trips with the technicians to see what they did and to understand why we ordered certain parts. That was so much fun, I knew I wanted to move up to be a technician.

What kind of preparation did you have?
I didn't have any special education or training for the customer service or dispatcher jobs. But before I was promoted to technician, I took a 15-week course at the Metropolitan Institute of Network Technology in New Jersey to learn all about telecommunications networking.

What was the hardest aspect of working in the field during your first few years?
I got a lot of network theory in the technical program, but I really didn't start learning until I got my hands on the equipment. So at first I had a lot to learn.

How long did it take you to get established?
It took about two and a half months to feel comfortable at the technician job.

What do you currently do?
I'm in charge of making sure all the feeds of Dow Jones's international network are up at all times. I work in the data center, looking at terminals to see what is happening with the different connections. I also do installations of cables, modems and monitors in the building, and I set up local area networks.

What do you like most about your work?
I like the fact that my job is hands on. I used to do a lot of work on my car, and I always liked tinkering with stuff. I like doing something for the customer.

What do you like least?
The hard part is you always have to learn something new. There is always bigger and better equipment, and you have to pick up the manual and learn about it.

What has been your proudest achievement?
I'm proud that I got to where I am now. I wasn't too sure
that the computer field was going to be for me, but I found
I could pick everything up and go with it. I can figure stuff
out on my own.

**What advice would you offer someone who's thinking
about entering this field?**
You should try to take some specific courses in data communications because you could get a big jump-start there.
You should make sure that you get hands-on training if you
go to a trade school. But you aren't going to get anywhere
if you aren't motivated because it's a pretty competitive
business.

Ed Higgins, 27,
network control technician,
Weyerhaeuser Company,
Tacoma, Washington
Years in the business: three

How did you break into the field?
In the Marine Corps I was a radar technician for four years.
It was good training but highly specialized—how many
companies need radar technicians? So when I got out, I got
an associate degree in electronic technology in North Carolina. I thought that would help me get a foot in the door
somewhere. I responded to an ad in the paper for a job at
Dow Jones and was hired.

What did you do on your first job?
Dow Jones had a lot of subscribers to its financial network,
and we also did third-party maintenance for a different
company, Bloomberg and Telerate, that had its own equipment. I traveled by car to do parts changing, fax machine
hookups and a lot of installations with modems.

When we were doing maintenance on the Telerate stock
quote equipment, we would go in to brokerage and bank
offices and first make sure the telephone line was installed
properly. Then we would make sure the voltage levels were
correct and hook up a speaker to listen to the bits of data

coming across the line. If that was okay, we would connect a modular plug from there to the Telerate equipment. Then we would check the controller and the monitor and do some commands to bring up the screen and make sure they were getting the financial information over the line.

Was that a typical first job?
I think so. It didn't do much for my knowledge of data communications, but I got to see what a lot of the stuff was and how people used the different equipment.

What was the hardest aspect of working in the field during your first few years?
Hooking up the fax machines—they were a pain. The manuals were pretty sketchy, so you could be caught out in the field without knowing what you were doing. With third-party maintenance you're called out to work on stuff blind—it's often equipment you've never seen before.

What do you currently do?
We oversee all of the data communications between Weyerhaeuser's headquarters here and all of its sites around the world; I think there are more than 100 of them. We do a lot of modem testing, troubleshooting for communications problems, and in the future I think we're going to be doing installations of LANs out in the field.

What do you like most about your work?
I like the technical aspect the best—I do a lot of analysis. Also, the field is changing so quickly you don't have time to be bored at all. You can always find something new to learn.

What do you like least?
Sitting down as much as 90 percent of the day. After traveling 150 miles a day with Dow Jones, I get bored being in the same place all the time. And I really don't get to interact with different people except the others in the network.

What have been your proudest achievements?
In most cases I've been able to pick up everything quicker than expected. In my last job I was pretty much self-sufficient on the night shift; I didn't wake up my senior people with questions or problems in the middle of the night.

What advice would you offer someone who's thinking about entering this field?
It would help to have a year of telecommunications courses —a lot of community colleges are giving them—before going into the field. Or at least people should have some experience with computers or PCs. Sometimes you can get a foot in the door that way.

Stan Waldref, 47,
network systems programmer, Eddie Bauer, Redmond, Washington
Years in the business: 23

How did you break into the field?
Purely by accident. I was always interested in electronics as a kid; I liked working on cars and figuring out what was wrong. After high school I did a one-year electronics course in radio/TV broadcasting. Then I went into the Air Force. After four years in the service I went to work in Seattle for Western Electric, which was a subsidiary of AT&T, as a telecommunications installer. I worked there for five and a half years, and then I got laid off because business was down.

I decided to go to college and get a business administration degree, but after two years I stopped because I had started a family and wasn't making enough money in my part-time job. I got a job at Booth Computer in Seattle as a field engineer, working on the network side. After three months I was sent out in the field to troubleshoot, maintain and repair telecommunications equipment.

What did you do in your first job at Western Electric?
As an installer I'd go into a central office and mark where each bay for the new phone system would go. I'd put in all the hardware and equipment (e.g., monitors and printers), and then we'd move into wiring up all the different hardware. Then came the third phase, which was actually connecting the wires to the equipment in the designated area so they could access the equipment from the phones. Phase four was testing and troubleshooting the equipment to make

sure it was installed correctly and we could get a dial tone. Then we'd use electronic equipment that would exercise units to make sure they functioned properly. I wasn't working directly with computers, though.

When did you first get involved with data communication?

In my first computer job, at Booth, I worked on how the communications link between the office and its headquarters in Phoenix was brought up and what was needed to make that link work.

What was the hardest aspect of working in the field during your first few years?

Having the patience needed to move up and to become proficient in all of the phases. I wanted to learn too much too fast.

How long did it take you to get established?

About three months. It seemed to come easy for me. My first boss said he couldn't believe how quickly I picked it up. I was lucky to fall into what I enjoy doing.

How many different jobs have you held in this field?

I've had eight jobs: telecommunications installer for Western Electric; field engineer for Booth Computer in the computer room; field engineer outside the office for Booth in Seattle and then the Denver area; field engineer supervisor for Booth in Denver; network operator for First Bank of Denver; assistant to network programmer for Airborne Express in Seattle; network programmer for Airborne Express; and now, network systems programmer for Eddie Bauer.

What do you currently do?

Eddie Bauer has retail stores and catalog sales. I put different definitions into network programs to bring outside users into our mainframe system to access information. I identify items needed to accomplish this and try to organize it so it all goes together at the appropriate time to get the people on line. I use modems, phone lines and whatever hardware is needed on both the host and the user ends to make the connection work.

What do you like most about your work?

That it's a constantly changing environment. Everything is revolving, new things happen from day to day. You can see your accomplishments immediately. When I get a problem, I can fix it and see the results right away.

What do you like least?

I learned that being in management isn't fun for me. When I was a supervisor in Colorado, I asked to be demoted back to field engineer because I was on the road from dawn until dusk or later, and I rarely had time with my family.

What has been your proudest achievement?

The fact that I can be responsive to user needs. If they have a problem, I can go in and fix it in a minimum amount of time, and I can present a cost-saving approach to my employer.

What advice would you offer someone who's thinking about entering this field?

If you want to move up—and if you're not going to get college training—you've got to be aggressive. You've got to have a "willing to put in hours" attitude. If you can show that drive and an aggressive approach to learning and problem solving, you can move up in the field fast.

WILL YOU FIT INTO THE COMPUTER INDUSTRY?

Before you enroll in a program of study or start to search for a job in one of the careers described in this book, it's smart to figure out whether that career is a good fit, given your background, skills and personality. There are a number of ways to do this. They include:

❑ Talk to people who work in that field. Find out what they like and don't like about their jobs, what kinds of people their employers hire and what their recommendations are about training.

❑ Use a computer to help you identify career options. Some of the most widely used programs are *Discover*, by the American College Testing Service, *SIGI Plus*, developed by the Educational Testing Service, and *Career Options* by Peterson's. Some public libraries make this career software available to library users at low or no cost. The career counseling or guidance offices of your high school or local community college are other possibilities.

❑ Take a vocational interest test. The most commonly used tests are the Strong-Campbell Interest Inventory and the Kuder Occupational Interest Survey. High schools and colleges usually offer free testing to their students and alumni through their guidance and career-planning offices. Many career counselors in private practice and those at community job centers are also trained to interpret results.

81

❑ Consult a career counselor. You can find one by asking friends and colleagues if they know of any good ones. Or contact the career information office of the adult education division of a local college. Its staff and workshop leaders often do one-on-one counseling. The job information services division of major libraries sometimes offers low- or no-cost counseling by appointment. Or check the *Yellow Pages* under the heading ''Vocational Guidance.''

Before you spend time, energy or money doing any of the above, take one or more of the following five quizzes (one for each career described in the book). The results can help you decide whether you really are cut out to work in a particular career.

If becoming a computer service technician interests you, take this quiz:

Read each statement, then choose the number 0, 5 or 10. The rating scale below explains what each number means.

> **0** = Disagree
> **5** = Agree somewhat
> **10** = Strongly agree

____I have always been a tinkerer

____I am a good listener and don't mind asking questions to get more information

____I am good at figuring out why something is not working properly

____I have good powers of observation

____I have a good basic understanding of computer hardware, software and operating systems

____I enjoy keeping up with the latest in computer technology

____Working under pressure doesn't rattle me

____My math skills are good

____I am handy working with small tools and parts

____I can stay calm and be soothing when dealing with people who are upset

Now add up your score.   ___Total points

If your total points were less than 50, you probably do not have sufficient interest or inclination to learn what's required to become a computer service technician. If your total points were between 50 and 75, you may have what it takes to get into computer repair, but be sure to do more investigation by following the suggestions at the beginning of this section. If your total points were 75 or more, it's highly likely that you are a good candidate to work in the field of computer service.

If computer operations interests you, take this quiz:

Read each statement, then choose the number 0, 5 or 10. The rating scale below explains what each number means.

0 = Disagree
5 = Agree somewhat
10 = Strongly agree

___I am good at following directions precisely
___When something stops working, I like trying to figure out what went wrong
___I am not intimidated by the prospect of being the person responsible for something important
___I am a methodical and highly organized type of person
___I can work with little supervision
___I am capable of sitting at a computer terminal for hours
___I prefer working in a relaxed work environment
___I don't mind working unconventional work hours
___I can remain calm and think clearly when I'm in a stressful situation
___I like the idea of working with mainframe computers

Now add up your score.   ___Total points

If your total points were 50 or less, you probably do not have sufficient interest or inclination to learn what's required to become a computer and peripheral operator. If your total points were between 50 and 75, you may have what it takes to get into mainframe operations, but be sure to do more investigation by following the suggestions at the beginning of this section. If your total points were 75 or above, it's highly likely that you are a good candidate for working with mainframe systems in a data processing department.

If becoming a desktop publisher interests you, take this quiz:

Read each statement, then choose the number 0, 5 or 10. The rating scale below explains what each number means.

0 = Disagree
5 = Agree somewhat
10 = Strongly agree

____I know or would like to learn about page layout, design and typography

____I have good eye-hand coordination

____I know or would like to learn desktop publishing software programs

____I don't mind working under the pressure of deadlines

____I have a good sense of design

____I like working as a member of a team on projects

____I pay a lot of attention to details to make sure I get things perfect

____I have good listening and verbal skills

____I can visualize in my head how I would like printed information to appear in its final form

____I can spend hours working on a personal computer without getting tired or bored

Now add up your score.   ____Total points

If your total points were less than 50, you probably do not have sufficient interest or inclination to learn what's required to go into desktop publishing. If your total points were between 50 and 75, you may have what it takes to get into desktop publishing, but be sure to do more investigation by following the suggestions at the beginning of this section. If your total points were 75 or more, it's highly likely that you are a good candidate to work as a desktop publisher.

If becoming a retail computer salesperson interests you, take this quiz:

Read each statement, then choose the number 0, 5 or 10. The rating scale below explains what each number means.

0 = Disagree
5 = Agree somewhat
10 = Strongly agree

___I like keeping up-to-date with the newest computer models

___I enjoy showing people how different computers and software work

___I feel comfortable striking up conversations with people I don't know

___I don't take it personally if people tell me "No"

___I have an upbeat, positive attitude

___I can maintain my cool with difficult or rude people

___I enjoy talking about computers and software with people

___I have good basic math skills and can use a calculator

___I am familiar with or would like to learn the most popular software programs

___I can be persuasive without being off-putting

Now add up your score.   ___Total points

If your total points were less than 50, you probably do not have sufficient interest or inclination to learn what's required to become a computer salesperson. If your total points were between 50 and 75, you may have what it takes to get into computer sales, but be sure to do more investigation by following the suggestions at the beginning of this section. If your total points were 75 or more, it's highly likely that you are a good candidate to work in the field of retail computer sales.

If telecommunications interests you, take this quiz:

Read each statement, then choose the number 0, 5 or 10. The rating scale below explains what each number means.

0 = Disagree
5 = Agree somewhat
10 = Strongly agree

___I have good listening skills

___I can be reassuring to people who are upset because they are experiencing a problem

___I can pick up or move boxes that might weigh as much as 80 pounds

___When it comes to solving a problem I can be very persistent

___I enjoy working with computers and always want to learn more about new equipment and programs

___My reading and comprehension skills are very good

___I am handy with small tools

___I am familiar with or would like to learn more about data communications

___I have always been a tinkerer

___Setting up computer equipment and making sure it's working right is something that gives me satisfaction

Now add up your score.   ___Total points

If your total points were less than 50, you probably do not have sufficient interest or inclination to learn what's required to become a telecommunications technician. If your total points were between 50 and 75, you may have what it takes to get into telecommunications, but be sure to do more investigation by following the suggestions at the beginning of this section. If your total points were 75 or more, it's highly likely that you are a good candidate to work in the field of telecommunications.

ABOUT THE AUTHOR

Linda Williams is a reporter for the *Puget Sound Business Journal* in Seattle, Washington. She has written freelance articles on technology, business and other subjects for many publications, including *American Way, Careers, Euromoney, Sunset, Home Office Computing, Washington CEO* and the *Seattle Weekly.* Williams was formerly a reporter for *Time* magazine in New York and covered subjects ranging from computers to arts and entertainment. She has a master's degree in journalism from Columbia University and a BA in journalism and literature from Indiana University.